Snap books®

Favorite
HORSES
Breeds Girls Love

by Molly Kolpin

Consultant:
Jennifer Zablotny, DVM
American Veterinary Medical Association
Michigan Veterinary Medical Association

CAPSTONE PRESS
a capstone imprint

Snap Books are published by Capstone Press,
1710 Roe Crest Drive, North Mankato, Minnesota 56003
www.capstonepub.com

Library of Congress Cataloging-in-Publication Data
Kolpin, Molly, author.
Favorite horses : breeds girls love / by Molly Kolpin.
pages cm. — (Snap books. Crazy about horses)
Summary: "Photos and text introduce readers to different
horse breeds, including specific breed characteristics,
features, and origins"— Provided by publisher.
Audience: Ages 8–14.
Audience: Grades 4 to 6.
Includes bibliographical references and index.
ISBN 978-1-4914-0708-0 (library binding)
ISBN 978-1-4914-0714-1 (eBook PDF)
1. Horse breeds—Juvenile literature. 2. Horses—Juvenile
literature. I. Title.
SF291.K65 2015
636.1—dc23   2014005282

Editorial Credits
Michelle Hasselius, editor; Juliette Peters and
Kazuko Collins, designers; Deirdre Barton, media
researcher; Laura Manthe, production specialist

Photo Credits
© 2004 Mark J. Barrett, 10, 11 (top); American Morgan Horse
Association, 11 (bottom), 25 (t); Getty Images Inc: and, 9,
Elsa, 15, Matthew Stockman, 14; Shutterstock: Aleksandra
Aleksandrova, 2–3, Alexia Khruscheva, 6, 13, anakondasp,
25 (b), Anastasiia Golovkova, 3 (br), 30, andersphoto, tooled
floral pattern leather design, donatas1205, brown leather
square design, ebubekir olcok, 28 (t), Eduard Kyslynskyy, 1,
eliz, 21 (t), Gregory Johnston, 22 (right), gurinaleksandr, 7
(t), jonbraid, 26, Lenkadan, 8, lightbeserk, 29 (t), Marakova
Viktoria, 4, Margo Harrison, 27, Nicole Ciscato, 19 (tr),
23 (b), nuttakit, brown leather strip design, Olga_i, 5 (b),
outdoorsman, 28 (b), Papava, 22 (left), Paula Cobleigh, 19
(b), Perry Corell, 24, Peter38, 23 (t), photowings, 31, pirita,
5 (m), 12, Reinhold Leitner, wood design, Teri Virbickis, 32,
thinz, vertical stripe design, floral designs, Vera Zinkova, 19
(mr), Winthrop Brookhouse, 7 (b), Zuzule, cover (horse), 5
(t), 16, 17, 18, 19 (tl, tm, bl, br), 20, 21 (b), 29 (b)

Glossary terms are bolded on first use in text.

Printed in the United States of America in North Mankato, Minnesota.
032014   008087CGF14

TABLE of CONTENTS

BREED *Basics*

From the Appaloosa's colorful coat to the Clydesdale's incredible strength, every horse **breed** has its own claim to fame. Surprisingly most modern-day horse breeds' unique features did not happen by accident. Humans created different horse breeds for specific reasons. Some horses were bred to move at breathtaking speeds. Others were bred to help farmers and cattle ranchers with their work.

To the untrained eye, it can be difficult to tell different horse breeds apart. But horse-loving girls make it their mission to know every feature of their favorite breeds.

WHICH BREED IS BEST?

When choosing a horse, it's important to pick a breed that fits the owner's needs. See what breed you'd pick by filling in the blanks below.

Appaloosa

I love horses that are _____ .
a. strong   **b.** fast   **c. versatile**
My ideal horse would be able to _____ .
a. pull heavy loads   **b.** race
c. go on trail rides
Horses that _____ are my favorite.
a. are very large
b. have fiery **temperaments**
c. need to be trained to carry riders

If your answers were mostly "a," a Percheron or Clydesdale is best for you. If you answered mostly "b," a Thoroughbred is your breed. If your answers were mostly "c," your best match is probably a quarter horse, Morgan, Appaloosa, or paint horse.

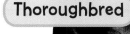
Thoroughbred

WHERE IT ALL BEGAN

Arabian

The world's oldest breed of horse is the Arabian. This striking horse is the source of all other breeds. The Bedouins of the Arabian Desert developed the breed centuries ago. They needed a horse with stamina to carry them across the desert plains. Arabians are now renowned throughout the world for their strength, **endurance**, intelligence, beauty, and gentle natures.

All-AMERICAN
Classics

Today the United States is home to more horses than any other country in the world. But horse numbers weren't always so high. Scientists believe the horse's earliest ancestors originated in North America and then spread to other continents. Over time all the prehistoric horses in America eventually died out. Then in the 1700s, Spanish explorers reintroduced horses to America. The small, robust horses they brought over on ships were called Colonial Spanish horses.

It wasn't long before horses became an important part of American culture. American Indians rode horses when hunting buffalo. Western cowboys rode horses when herding and roping cattle. Soldiers even rode horses into battle during times of war. Over the years dedicated horse lovers developed their own all-American breeds.

HORSES ON THE MOVE

Wondering how America's earliest horses made it across the ocean to Europe and Asia? Here's a hint—they didn't swim. Instead they crossed what is now known as the Bering Strait. Millions of years ago, this area of water between Alaska and Russia didn't exist. The two landmasses were connected, and horses simply walked across!

DID YOU KNOW?

America's wild mustangs descend from the horses brought over by Spanish explorers.

mustang

7

Quarter HORSE

Strong, sturdy, smart, and fast, the quarter horse is recognized as the world's most popular breed. These horses stand about 15 to 16 hands high. Their muscular frames contain large quarters that give the horses their speed. But don't think the name quarter horse comes from their giant quarters. The name actually refers to the quarter-mile races these horses once participated in. Quarter horses can reach speeds up to 55 miles (89 kilometers) per hour when **sprinting**!

There are still a few quarter-mile races held in the United States today. But today quarter horses are known more for their herding skills than for their short-distance sprinting abilities. Their agility and control, combined with their intelligence, make them ideal horses for roping cattle. They quickly became the favorite breed of countless cowboys and cowgirls working on the Western frontier.

BREED BEGINNINGS

The quarter horse isn't just the most popular American horse breed. It's also the oldest. Early settlers began developing the quarter horse in the 1600s. They bred both English and Spanish horses to create the breed.

DID YOU KNOW?

Horses are measured in hands. One hand equals 4 inches (10 centimeters). A horse is measured from its hooves to the top of its **withers**.

The quarter horse came from Spanish origins, like these Andalusians.

MORGAN

All modern-day Morgans are related to a single **stallion** named Justin Morgan. Justin Morgan was born in Massachusetts in 1789. He became legendary in his time for his unmatched strength and stamina.

Today's Morgans display the same strength and stamina that made their **forefather** famous. These horses are intelligent and spirited, but easy to control and gentle around children. Morgans typically stand between 14.2 and 15.2 hands high. Most have coats that are chestnut, bay, brown, or black in color. They also have silky manes and tails.

Morgans were especially bred for pleasure and have many uses for today's horse enthusiasts. Their intelligence and athletic abilities help them excel in competitions such as **dressage** and endurance riding. Morgans are also an ideal horse for casual trail rides. The Morgan is up to the challenge of almost any activity.

POWERFUL GENES

Most **foals** display characteristics from both parents. But Justin Morgan's **offspring** always took after him. Generations of Morgans have continued to pass on the stallion's physical and behavioral traits.

Morgan foal

DID YOU KNOW?

Justin Morgan was originally named Figure. Later he was renamed Justin Morgan after his owner.

Justin Morgan

LIGHTNING-FAST
Thoroughbreds

Known to be the fastest long-distance horse in the world, the Thoroughbred rules the racetrack. This breed's body was made for speed. Long, strong legs provide power. A deep chest allows the horse's lungs to expand when breathing heavily. Physical features like these help the Thoroughbred reach speeds of 43 miles (69 km) per hour.

ARABIAN INFLUENCE

Thoroughbreds were developed in England about 300 years ago with three Arabian **sires**. These Arabians were the Byerley Turk, the Darley Arabian, and the Godolphin Arabian.

The Thoroughbred's speed is matched by a fiery spirit. In fact some Thoroughbreds have rather challenging temperaments. These horses are extremely courageous and bold. Though sometimes difficult to control, their daring natures can be an advantage on the racetrack.

Thoroughbreds are not only renowned for their speed and spirit, but also for their beauty. Most Thoroughbreds stand 16 to 16.2 hands high. Their shiny coats are generally brown, chestnut, black, or gray. They currently reign as one of the world's most popular breeds.

ACING *the* RACES

Every year on the first Saturday in May, millions tune in to watch the Kentucky Derby. The Kentucky Derby is one of the most famous horse races in the world and is only for 3-year-old Thoroughbreds. At the Churchill Downs racetrack in Louisville, more than 100,000 people gather on Derby day. It's tradition for Derby goers to dress up in fancy clothing. Women wear large, elaborate hats.

When the race starts, a deafening roar rises from the crowd. Everyone is excited to cheer on his or her favorite Thoroughbred. The race is just 1.25 miles (2 km) long. But in that short distance, the racehorses display incredible speeds.

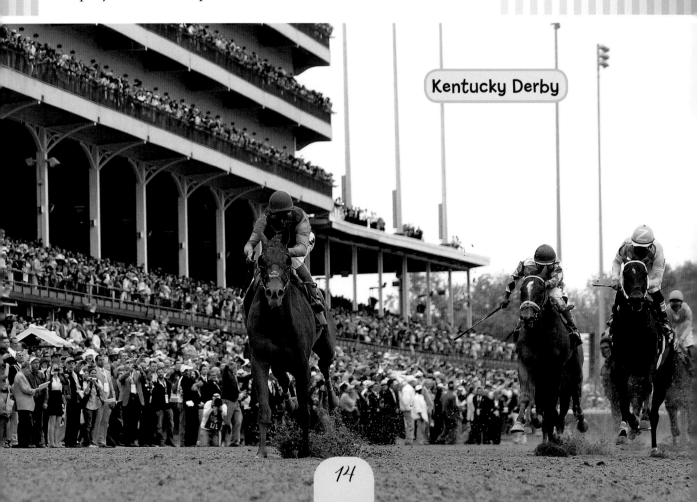

Kentucky Derby

DID YOU KNOW?

The Kentucky Derby has been held at Churchill Downs every year since 1875.

The winner of the Kentucky Derby has the chance to become a Triple Crown winner. Winning the Triple Crown requires first place in three races—the Kentucky Derby, Preakness Stakes, and Belmont Stakes. Thoroughbreds that manage to earn the Triple Crown gain immediate, lifelong fame.

PATTERNED *Beauties*

Some horse breeds are known for their strength or speed. But the Appaloosa and paint horse are known for their colorful coats. Both of these breeds come from horses brought to America by Spanish explorers. American Indians are responsible for developing the two breeds.

The Appaloosa and paint horse have many similarities. Both have compact bodies and strong muscles built for power. But differences exist between the two breeds.

THE NAME GAME

When different groups of people first saw horses, they needed names to describe them. American Indians came up with "big dog," "holy dog," and "elk dog." Hawaiians called horses "canoes that travel on land." Australians called them "the newcomer's kangaroo."

DID YOU KNOW?

A horse was once a sign of wealth among American Indian tribes.

Most Appaloosas are slightly smaller than the average paint horse. They also have thin, wispy manes. They are extremely intelligent but prone to stubbornness. Paint horses are calm and easygoing.

For American Indians, it was the Appaloosa and paint horse's patterned coats that made them especially valuable. The patterns helped these horses blend in with their surroundings. American Indians riding paint horses or Appaloosas could better sneak up on their enemies. Today both breeds make the list of America's top 10 most popular horse breeds.

APPALOOSA

Appaloosa fans can thank the Nez Perce tribe for the creation of this colorful breed. The Nez Perce lived in the Pacific Northwest. They began breeding Appaloosas in the 1700s. Tribe members needed a horse that could handle long hunts and mountainous terrain. They bred Appaloosas to be intelligent, sensible, and athletic. These traits, along with the Appaloosa's beautiful coat, make them popular horses today.

The Appaloosa's athletic abilities help it excel in both jumping and racing. Thanks to their striking appearance, many Appaloosas have even appeared in circuses and parades. This is one horse that truly has the best of both worlds—beauty and brains.

COOL COATS

Appaloosas have five different coat patterns.

snowflake

white spots on the body and hips

blanket

white on the hips, with or without dark spots

leopard

white on the sides and hips with dark spots

frost

white flecks on a dark coat

marble

light coat covered with dark flecks

Palouse River in Washington

DID YOU KNOW?

Appaloosas are named after the Palouse River. This river runs through the states of Washington and Idaho, where the Nez Perce once lived.

PAINT *Horse*

It's easy to see how the paint horse got its name. These horses look as if a bucket of paint was splashed on their bodies. Unlike the Appaloosa, which has small speckles, the paint horse has large patches of color.

The most common type of coloring for a paint horse is tobiano. Tobiano horses have white coats with dark patches. Overo horses have dark coats with white patches. Sabino is a special term for horses that have white markings starting on their legs and running up their bodies. Splashed white describes paint horses that are largely covered in white with dark patches that have smooth edges.

American Indians living in the central plains brought this breed fame. Soon cowboys and pioneers also fell in love with the paint horse's calm and steady nature. This horse is happy just about anywhere, whether on the trail or in the ring.

PINTO VS. PAINT

Many people think pintos and paint horses are the same breed. But the pinto isn't a breed at all. A pinto is any horse with a two-colored coat. Paint horses, however, must meet actual breed standards.

DID YOU KNOW?

A paint horse's skin has the same color patches as its coat.

HEAVY *Lifters*

About 1,500 years ago, a Chinese invention forever changed the lives of horses and humans. The invention was a padded collar that could be placed around a horse's neck. With these collars horses could be used to pull wagons, plows, and timber. Forests could be cleared faster than ever before, and farmers were able to harvest more crops.

But not just any horse could be used to pull such heavy loads. Only the world's strongest, heaviest, and most powerful horses were equipped for such tasks. Two of these horses are still famous today—the Percheron and the Clydesdale.

MACHINES TAKE THE REINS

By the 1950s and 1960s, machines had replaced almost all of the heavy horses' jobs. The demand for heavy horses plummeted. Some heavy horse breeds nearly became **extinct**. Today heavy horse breeds such as the Suffolk are still struggling to regain their numbers.

DID YOU KNOW?

Heavy horses used for pulling are often referred to as draft horses.

Suffolk

23

PERCHERON

The Percheron was developed in France and is known as one of the world's most versatile breeds. Gifted with incredible strength, Percherons are ideal horses for pulling heavy farm equipment. But that's not all these horses can do. They have also been used as warhorses and coach horses. Percherons have even been saddled up and ridden for pleasure. Their grace, intelligence, and calm temperaments make Percherons suitable for many different purposes.

Percherons stand between 16 and 17.2 hands high. They have deep chests and extremely muscular legs. Most Percherons are gray or black with thick manes. These hardy, easygoing giants are extremely popular. They have been sold all over the world.

The largest Percheron on record was named Dr. LeGear. Born in 1902 Dr. LeGear stood 21 hands high and weighed 3,024 pounds (1,372 kilograms). The world record for the smallest horse goes to Thumbelina, a miniature horse that stands 4.4 hands high and weighs 57 pounds (26 kg).

DID YOU KNOW?

Oriental and Spanish breeds were used to develop the Percheron. These breeds gave the Percheron its elegance and grace.

CLYDESDALE

Percherons may be one of the world's most versatile horses, but Clydesdales are the world's strongest. This breed was developed during the 1700s in Scotland by the sixth Duke of Hamilton and John Paterson. Both Flemish horses and Shires were used to develop the Clydesdale.

DID YOU KNOW?
A single Clydesdale once pulled a 50-ton (45-metric ton) load across a distance of 1,320 feet (402 meters)!

Clydesdales measure up to 16.2 hands high. Most are bay, brown, or black. Many have white markings on their legs and face, with heavy **feathering** on their large, broad hooves. They are recognized as friendly horses that are eager to please and quick to learn.

In the 1700s and 1800s, Clydesdales were used to pull heavy farm equipment in Great Britain. Like Percherons, they were so good at pulling heavy loads that they were sold all over the world. They are surprisingly active for their large size and have elegant ways of moving. Today Clydesdales are often seen pulling **carriages** in parades.

EQUINE QUIZ

How well do you know your horse breeds? Take this quiz to find out.

1. The Kentucky Derby is a horse race for 3-year-old _____.
   a. Morgans
   b. Thoroughbreds
   c. quarter horses
   d. Percherons

2. The Nez Perce tribe is responsible for developing the_____.
   a. paint horse
   b. quarter horse
   c. Appaloosa
   d. Morgan

3. The_____is named for the quarter-mile races it once competed in.
   a. Clydesdale
   b. paint horse
   c. Percheron
   d. quarter horse

4. Tobiano and overo are coat patterns for the_____.
   a. Thoroughbred
   b. Clydesdale
   c. Morgan
   d. paint horse

5. The biggest_____on record was born in 1902 and named Dr. LeGear.
   a. Clydesdale
   b. Percheron
   c. quarter horse
   d. Morgan

6. Justin Morgan is the sire responsible for today's_____.
   a. Thoroughbreds
   b. paint horses
   c. Morgans
   d. Appaloosas

7. Because of their extreme pulling abilities,_____were once sold all over the world.
   a. Clydesdales
   b. paint horses
   c. Thoroughbreds
   d. quarter horses

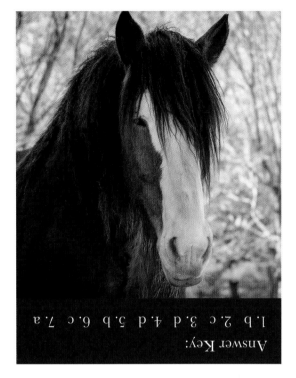

Answer Key:
1. b 2. c 3. d 4. d 5. b 6. c 7. a

DID YOU KNOW?

More than 100 horse breeds exist today.

GLOSSARY

breed (BREED)—a certain kind of animal within an animal group

carriage (KA-rij)—a vehicle with wheels that is pulled by horses

dressage (dre-SAHZH)—an equestrian sport in which a trained horse shows its ability to move precisely and gracefully based on cues from its rider

endurance (en-DUR-enss)—the ability to keep doing an activity for long periods of time

extinct (ik-STINGKT)—no longer living; an extinct animal is one that has died out with no more its kind

feathering (FETH-ur-ing)—long hair around a horse's legs and feet; only certain horse breeds have feathering

foal (FOHL)—a horse that is less than 1 year old

forefather (FOR-fah-thur)—the founder of a family

offspring (OF-spring)—animals born to a set of parents

sire (SY-ur)—the male parent of an animal

sprint (SPRINT)—to run fast for a short distance

stallion (STAL-yuhn)—an adult male horse that can be used for breeding

temperament (TEM-pur-uh-muhnt)—the combination of an animal's behavior and personality

versatile (VUR-suh-tuhl)—talented or useful in many ways

withers (WITH-urs)—the tops of a horse's shoulders

READ MORE

Behling, Silke. *Get to Know Horse Breeds: The 100 Best-Known Breeds.* Get to Know Cat, Dog, and Horse Breeds. Berkeley Heights, N.J.: Enslow Publishers, 2014.

Crosby, Jeff. *Harness Horses, Bucking Broncos & Pit Ponies: A History of Horse Breeds.* Toronto: Tundra Books, 2011.

Kolpin, Molly. *All About Horses: Everything a Horse-Crazy Girl Needs to Know.* Crazy About Horses. North Mankato, Minn.: Capstone Press, 2015.

INTERNET SITES

FactHound offers a safe, fun way to find Internet sites related to this book. All of the sites on FactHound have been researched by our staff.

Here's all you do:

Visit *www.facthound.com*

Type in this code: 9781491407080

INDEX